Meditation

by Sri Swami Satchidananda

Library of Congress Cataloging in
Publication Data
Satchidananda, Swami.
Meditation

I. Title.
2011
IBSN 0-932040-07-7

1st Printing: 1975
Revised Edition: 2011
2nd Printing: 2013

Printed in the United States of America.

Integral Yoga® Publications
Satchidananda Ashram–Yogaville, Inc.
108 Yogaville Way, Buckingham, VA, USA 23921
www.IntegralYoga.org

Integral Yoga® Publications
Yogaville, Virginia, USA

Books by
Sri Swami Satchidananda

Beyond Words

Enlightening Tales

The Golden Present

Bound To Be Free:
The Liberating Power
of Prison Yoga

The Healthy Vegetarian

Heaven on Earth

Integral Yoga Hatha

Kailash Journal

The Living Gita

To Know Your Self

Yoga Sutras of Patanjali

Titles in this special
Peter Max cover art series:

Meditation

The Key to Peace

Overcoming Obstacles

Adversity and Awakening

Satchidananda Sutras

Gems of Wisdom

Pathways to Peace

How to Find Happiness

The Be-Attitudes

Everything Will Come to You

Thou Art That:
How to Know Yourself

Free Yourself

The Guru Within

Books/Films about
Sri Swami Satchidananda

Sri Swami Satchidananda:
   Biography of a Yoga Master

Sri Swami Satchidananda:
   Portrait of a Modern Sage

The Master's Touch

Boundless Giving: The Life and Service of
Sri Swami Satchidananda

Living Yoga: The life and teachings of
   Swami Satchidananda (DVD)

Many Paths, One Truth: The Interfaith
   Message of Swami Satchidananda (DVD)

The Essence of Yoga:
   The Path of Integral Yoga with
   Swami Satchidananda (DVD)

For complete listing of books, CDs and DVDs:
www.iydbooks.com

Contents

Introduction

The aim of Yoga is to know the truth, which is one's Self. This knowledge alone can help us to free ourselves from all turmoil and petty mindedness.

We have a tendency to divide people into thousands of names: *I am this, I am that. Oh, he is different from me, she is different from me.* We group people by their color, by their country, by their race and by their religion; and we kill each other.

All this happens because we fail to see, to know, that we are above all these things. But if you reach into the depths of your own Self, you will find this contentment. By knowing your true nature, you will also know the truth in others. It is in that truth that we come together.

And it is this goal that is expounded, either directly or indirectly, in all the different religions and philosophies. To contemplate these points or to come to this realization within one's Self is what you call meditation. This realization is arrived at either directly or indirectly, according to the nature of the individual's practice.

The technique of meditation is to keep the mind fully occupied on one thing. When the mind is fully occupied on one thing, it is kept away from many things, and it becomes quiet. Then, you find a kind of calmness, and in that stillness even that one thing will slip away after some time.

It's something like going to sleep. You set aside all your work; you lie down in bed and you might listen to some soft, gentle music. If you really want to go to sleep, you don't think of anything else, aside from the music; and, after some time, even the music is forgotten.

Meditation is similar, except that we shouldn't become unconscious as we do in sleep. So, that process of sticking to one thing, concentrating on one thing, will slowly make you raise above that one thing also. In other words, when you concentrate fully on only one thing, that one thing will become nothing (no-thing). Then, you will realize everything by realizing your true Self.

Concentration should culminate in meditation. Meditation should slowly make you slip into *samadhi*, which you can call the transcendental level. In *samadhi*, you transcend the mind and body and enjoy your true nature.

The Process of Meditation

Meditation begins with concentration–trying to focus your mind on any one point. I say any one point, because that point can vary to suit the taste, temperament, habit and faith of the individual. One approach is that of self-analysis. Watch the mind and ask yourself: Whose thoughts are these? Who is worried? Who is troubled? Who is disturbed? Who am I then? How do I know all these things? My knowing doesn't seem to become disturbed when I know that I am disturbed.

The process, then, is to identify with the knower and not with the disturbances in the mind. This is direct analysis. Or, simply be still and watch. Be quiet and watch what is happening in the mind and body. Sitting and watching your thoughts and breath movements, just become aware of the subtle movements within you.

On the other hand, an indirect means of analysis is to take yourself to be the mind: I am disturbed because I am having all kinds of wants. I want this, I want that. Let me resign from everything. Let me offer everything to humanity or to God. You pray, "God, take away these disturbances; give me happiness, give me peace." Sit and pray wholeheartedly, realizing the full meaning of every word. This, also, is meditation.

Another way is neither asking for anything, nor analyzing but just keeping the mind on one point. This point, or object of meditation, can be either a sacred name, a mystic mantra, the cosmic syllable *OM*, or Amen, *OM Shanti*, *Hari OM*, etc., or it can be a form. As there is no particular form of God, you can approach God through any form you wish. If you concentrate on a physical, concrete form–Jesus, Buddha, Siva or Krishna–after a time, you can create a mental picture of that form. Or, if you do not want a particular human form through which to worship God, then you can have a visual image of the sun, the moon, the stars. You can see God, you can approach God in any way or form you like, because God is present everywhere and in every form.

When you are trying to keep your mind on that point, whether it be an idea, a word or a form, you will often see the mind running here and there. Whenever it runs and you become aware of it, bring the mind gently back to the point. In another few minutes, it might run to another idea; bring it back. This constant effort of bringing the mind back, again and again to the point, is what you call concentration. In Sanskrit it is called *dharana*. You have not fixed the mind yet; you are trying to fix it. If that fixing of the mind becomes a little longer, then you are approaching meditation. When concentration becomes perfect it is called meditation. But don't think that you are wasting your time if your mind is not fully controlled. No one has ever achieved meditation right away. I come across many people complaining, "My mind runs here and there; how can I meditate?" *That is the process of meditation.*

When you repeat a mantra, a sacred word, repeat it mentally. Try to feel the inner vibration by your mental repetition. To do that, you have to draw your mind completely inward, and, then, you will be able to hear the sound within. The sound is not only produced when you say it audibly; there is an inaudible sound–the inner voice–within you that you can hear. And sometimes in your meditation, you might see different colored lights. Take that vision, itself, as your object for concentration.

The Yoga scriptures say that you can even take a nice dream–perhaps, you've dreamt of something divine, or you've had a dream of sages and saints or a vision of God–as your object of meditation. So, you see, there is no one object for everyone.

Preparing the body for meditation is another important factor. In meditation, you are trying to keep the mind steady and one-pointed. To do that, you must begin with the body; you must try to keep the body steady. That is possible only when you make a firm decision, a *sankalpa*, that you are not going to move any part of the body until you finish the meditation. The moment your body hears this decision, it will obey you. But the decision has to be very strong. The emphasis that you put on it will be heard by every cell in your body. They should know that you are a very strong taskmaster; then, they won't complain. Imagine your mind and body as little children. When you want them to behave well, you must be a little firm.

In meditation, it is best to sit in a cross-legged posture, keeping the spine in an erect position. Beginners may find this type of posture easier if they put one or more pillows under the buttocks, sitting on the edge of the pillow. This will bring the knees closer to the floor. After a while, if you really find it difficult to continue sitting cross-legged, change a little, but don't make too many changes. If sitting like this is impossible, use a chair, but make sure that the spine is straight with the chest well spread out. Just relax the body; don't make it stiff. In making the body strong and steady, don't make it tense.

Let the mental vision be indrawn. Do not do much with the physical eyeballs, but let the mental eye turn inward. You can fix your mental gaze on one of the nerve centers of the spinal column that are called *chakras* or plexuses. The most common is the heart (*anahata chakra*) or the eyebrow center (*ajna chakra*).

Another form of meditation is to imagine that there is a candle burning in the lotus of the heart. Once the mind is deeply interested in meditation, you will be able to forget the body. Until then, sit in the same posture, keeping the body relaxed and the spine steady but not stiff. The breath must also be regulated. The breath is the binding factor; it binds the mind to the body. So, if the breath is regulated, the mind is also regulated. Calm, slow and steady breathing will keep the mind very calm.

It is best to be regular in practicing meditation. Stick to one object of concentration. Don't continually change. Try to have two sittings daily. The best times are before sunrise and at sunset. If this is not possible, sit as soon as you wake up in the morning and at night before retiring. Begin by sitting for fifteen minutes and gradually increase the time.

Meditation Techniques

Japa Yoga: Meditation with a Mantra

Japa, the practice of repetition of a mantra, focuses the mind, makes it one-pointed and leads it into meditation. In this calm state, the powerful forces that are stored up in the unconscious get released and raised up to the conscious or subconscious level.

The same revelations or realizations experienced by so many great souls are lying dormant within every one of us. When these are awakened by *japa* and meditation, the result is the condition of expanded awareness.

A mantra is a sound structure, of one or more syllables, that represents a particular aspect of the divine vibration. Sages in deep meditation heard these sounds while experiencing some aspect of the Truth or God. Mantras have been handed down as guides to spiritual aspirants through generations of spiritual masters.

Concentrated mental repetition of the mantra produces vibrations, within the individual's entire system, that are in tune with the divine vibration.

Practicing with a mantra is a simple but very efficient and direct approach. It is a method that utilizes sound vibrations. As we all know, the entire creation is nothing but sound vibrations. "In the beginning was the Word. The Word was with God. The Word was God," the *Bible* says.

Every scripture says something similar. The unmanifested essence of God is static, but with creation it begins to vibrate. That cosmic vibration is called the *pranava*.

Pranava means a humming sound. That hum is called the Word or the sound, and it is expressed vocally by *OM* or Amen or Ameen. However, the real *OM* is not even spoken.

The real *OM* is to be felt within, in deep meditation, as the humming of the cosmic vibration. This hum vibrates at different levels and gives rise to different forms, because sound vibrations create forms.

Even science says that. We and everything else in the universe are nothing but sound vibrations in different wavelengths. Every particle vibrates, because there are atoms in it, filled with the movement of electrons and protons. After practicing for a long time, you will be able to hear the *anahata*, or the inner sound. That inner sound is always there.

If you want to make sure that you are alive, just close your eyes and ears and try to listen within. If you don't hear that hum, know that you are gone! Everyone has that sound within. It is that sound that keeps you alive.

To commune with this cosmic sound is to have communion with what the different religions call God. You can call it anything you want: communion with God or Yoga (union) with God or union with Nature.

To have this communion, you have to vibrate on the same wave length as the vibration of the cosmic sound. You have to become a radio receiver and tune yourself to that wavelength. It is to affect this tuning that the mantra is repeated, first vocally, later silently, with lip movements, and in an advanced stage, completely mentally. When the tuning is complete, the energy flows into you and you get the divine music.

The easiest, simplest and best practice is mantra *japa*. In fact, almost every spiritual tradition practices mantra *japa*. Even if you don't have time for anything else, don't miss your mantra *japa*.

All other practices are supplementary, because mantra *japa* is a direct way to tune yourself to that cosmic vibration. You don't have to think of the meaning of the mantra; just focus on the vibration and think that the same vibration is being created in you. When the tuning is complete, the energy flows into you and you get the divine music.

Hari OM

OM is the basic vibration. It vibrates every cell in your body and brings peace. *OM* creates a special rhythm in your system. You are sent into an ecstatic mood just by chanting *OM*. Of course, when you add *Hari* (*Ha* pronounced as the "ho" in hot, *ri* as the "re" in repeat), you get an added effect. *Hari* is another name for the Absolute. It means "the one that removes all obstacles, the one that purifies the entire system."

Repeating the word *Hari* makes you do a particular type of *pranayama,* or breathing exercise. Each syllable has its own significance. The first syllable, *Ha*, requires a contraction of the solar plexus. It creates a kind of *kapalabhati,* or bellows-breathing vibration, and it ignites the vast storehouse of physical and emotive power at the solar plexus.

In pronouncing *ri*, the system relaxes, and the throat contracts to make the force more concentrated. *Ri* brings in a special kind of heat. Then for *O*, the throat opens and the energy or sound rises upward from deep within the chest.

With the prolonged *Mmm*, the mouth closes and the energy goes to the head with a strong humming vibration. So *Hari* accelerates the system first, and the *OM* takes you to a higher level.

Repeat *Hari OM* in a monotone for as long as you feel comfortable. You can vary the pitch, speed and intensity according to the condition of the mind and, eventually, let the voice flow into silent repetition. After some time, just sit quietly and see how you are and what you feel.

OM Shanti

Shanti (Peace) is the nature of God. I see God as *Shanti*. God has no form, has no other name. God is all peaceful. God is all serenity. It is to be felt, it is to be experienced within one's self. When you are in peace, you are in God. You are with God.

Sit comfortably with the entire weight of the body supported by a straight spine. Observe your breathing, slowly making it deeper and deeper. Take long, slow, deep breaths, carefully observing the flow of the air in and out.

Follow the breath as it goes in; feel that it goes right through the spinal column to the base of the spine and then returns upward to the crown of the head when you exhale. After doing this a few times, let the breath flow in and out by itself without using any force.

After watching the breath for a few minutes, mentally repeat *OM* with the next incoming breath. Let the air flow in with the *OM* sound, and when it comes out, let it say *Shanti.*

Do not consciously do the breathing, but just be conscious of the breath and combine it with *OM Shanti.* Imagine the air flows in saying *OM* and rolls out with *Shanti.* You need not repeat it; just feel it.

This technique can be used with your own personal mantra or any mantra of your choosing. Combine the mantra with the breath in any way that is comfortable for you—splitting the mantra between the incoming and outgoing breath, or doing one repetition with the inhalation and another with the exhalation.

If you watch carefully, you will not only feel the air saying the chant or mantra, but you can listen to that. That needs complete attention, an indrawn mind. All through, keep the spine erect so that the flow will be easy.

Let the *OM* breath go deep to strike at the base of the spine, and then, with *Shanti,* let it roll upward through the spine to the crown of the head.

Thus, you will be feeling the air, or the breath, going in and out or downward and upward along the spine without its even flowing outside–you should try not to feel the air flowing outside through the nostrils but along the spine.

In the beginning, if you find it difficult to follow the breath up and down the spine in this way, then just follow the breath in and out of the body.

After a few months' practice, when you become comfortable with that, then begin to follow the breath along the spine. Try to keep the entire mind on the breath and the chant.

If you carefully observe the path along the spine, you will be able to feel a very mild heat, a gentle warmth that is very pleasant. Try not to miss that; put your entire attention on it.

The purpose of this practice of following the breath along the spine is to become conscious of the psychic energy traveling along the spine, passing through certain spiritual centers called *chakras*. However, it is inadvisable to keep the mind focused on the lower *chakras*.

If you become aware of a sensation of warmth there, feel it, but don't allow the mind to become fixed there. Bring the mind to one of the higher centers, such as the heart or eyebrow center, and draw the energy upward.

Continue to watch the breath, repeating *OM Shanthi* for as long as you feel comfortable. Then, to come out of meditation, slowly increase the duration of the inhalation and the exhalation. Make the breath longer and feel the air flowing out through the nostrils. Inhale and exhale deeply a few more times.

Carry this peaceful feeling from meditation all through the day, all through the week and all through your life. Even in the midst of a busy life, you can retain this peace.

Learn to do that; then, it will make no difference whether you are in a church or in the stock market. You can be in peace, at ease. Then it's only a matter of expanding–it's limitless. May this peace and joy prevail in your life always.

Mala Beads: An Additional Aid to *Japa*

The *japa mala* is a string of 108 beads with a mount bead called the *meru*. The *mala* is a physical aid to concentration. To use the *mala*, allow it to rest on your ring finger. Use the middle finger and the thumb to move the beads. Do not use the index finger. Let the *meru* be inside the moving fingers.

Push the beads inward one at a time with each repetition. Upon reaching the *meru*, do not cross over it, but turn the *mala* around and start again. The *mala* helps you not to fall into *laya,* or loss of awareness.

Ajapa-japa

Ajapa-japa is concentration upon the natural sound of the breath, which continually repeats the mantra *soham*. Relax your body. Sit comfortably so that you will not have to move for a while. Try to keep your spine erect, chest a little spread out and feel the weight of your body right on your seat. Find the center of gravity and just be relaxed.

Close your eyes. Concentrate on your breath and begin to breathe deeply; exhale fully and inhale deeply a few times. Have slow and deep exhalations and inhalations.

Let the mind follow the breath; forget the entire outside world and let the total awareness be on your breath now. Slowly, we are going to go into the very source of the individual personality. Do not put any effort into your breathing, but just allow the breath to flow normally. The breath may become very shallow, but continue to follow it.

Listen to your breath. If you listen carefully, you will be able to hear the sound *soham* (the "a" in "*ham*" is pronounced as the "u" in "up"). *So* when the breath flows in, *ham* when the breath flows out. It may be difficult in the beginning to hear the sound, but as the attention gets drawn inward, you will hear the breath repeating *soham*.

You need not repeat it yourself–just listen to the breath and you will be able to hear that sound. After practicing this for some time, you may begin to hear a humming musical note within you. Constantly listen to this hum. This is part of the cosmic vibration.

By concentrating on this inner vibration, you are in tune with the cosmic sound. That is why you are able to feel peace and bliss. Let there be a complete void, except for this musical note. By remaining in this state, you are sending out powerful peace vibrations that travel all over the globe and influence other minds, even restless minds.

In this very high state of silence, we have forgotten all our differences; we feel that we are One. You will be feeling very light; you will have transcended your body and you will feel that you have expanded and lost your individuality temporarily to be one with the cosmic mind.

After sitting for some time in silence, slowly direct your attention toward your breathing and gently make the breath a little deeper. Continue to deepen the breath for a few minutes and then close the meditation with chants:

Asato Ma Sad Gamaya
Tamaso Ma Jyothir Gamaya
Mrityor Mamritam Gamaya

Lead us from unreal to Real
Lead us from darkness to Light
Lead us from death to Immortality

OM Shanti, Shanti, Shanti
OM Peace, Peace, Peace

Loka Samasta Sukino Bhavanthu
May the entire universe be filled with peace and joy.

Meditation on a Form or Visual Symbol

The mind can be steadied by practicing repeated concentration and meditation on a visual form. The particular form can differ according to the individual's temperament and taste. Some examples are: the steady flame of a candle, a picture of a beloved saint or teacher, the symbol *OM*, a *yantra,* etc.

Form meditation usually begins with *tratak,* or steady gazing at the physical picture of the form. As you practice this, you may simultaneously repeat your chosen mantra. This steady gazing progresses into clear mental visualization of the object of concentration. An example of form meditation is given below.

A *yantra* is a mystic symbol in the form of a geometric diagram. Those who went into deep meditation experienced something in the unconscious levels of the mind.

Upon returning to normal consciousness, they expressed what they had experienced in the form of mantras, or mystic sounds, and *yantra*s.

This *yantra* is a diagram of the cosmos. The dot in the center represents the absolute consciousness. The surrounding circles are the subtle expressions of the three forces of nature which begin to manifest as the *yantra* spreads outward.

To practice meditation with the *yantra*, begin by having a picture of it in front of you at eye level. Gently gaze at it, holding the main part of the attention on the central dot. Do not strain the eyes. After some time, close the eyes and visualize the form mentally.

When visualization becomes difficult, open the eyes and practice the gentle gazing again. Start by gazing for just a few minutes and then gradually increase your practice. After some months, the visualization will become easy and your meditation will go deeper.

Self-Inquiry Meditation

This is purely a search within you.

Sit comfortably. Be fully relaxed. Then, start asking yourself, "Who am I?"

If the answer is, "I am Mr. Smith," ask yourself, "How and when did I get this name?'"

The answer might be, "My parents gave it to me as soon as I was born."

"Then, who were you before they gave you this name?"

"I was just a baby."

"If you were a baby then, who are you now?"

"A grown-up."

"Who grew up?"

"Well, my body."

"Not you?"

"Hmm ... this is rather puzzling."

Anything that you call *yours* is not you. In the above case, you are the subject and the body is the object. You are the passenger of the body, but you are not the body. Only when you identify yourself with the body do you speak of yourself as a baby, a grown-up, fat, slim, sick or healthy.

It is the same with respect to your mind. When you identify yourself with it, you call yourself a doctor, an engineer, a teacher or a student. You say you are happy, sorry, angry, etc., according to the modifications of the mind or the knowledge it has acquired. With all of these intrusions, there is confusion between you and something of yours.

Practice negating all you call yours. Witness each thought that comes and question yourself:

"To whom does this thought come?"

"To me."

"Who am I?"

Remain as a witness to the thoughts. Try to stand apart from these thoughts. This detachment is called *vairagya*.

When you can remain a witness and are not tossed by the waves in the mind, then you are in the state of *nirvana*– isolation or liberation. In this condition; you resemble the real Self and experience Oneness with it.

A Personal Experience

During a discussion period one Sunday afternoon, a young man asked Swami Satchidananda (Sri Gurudev) about an experience he had had in meditation.

"I have been practicing meditation by repeating my mantra and trying to feel that the Guru is seated on the crown of my head. One day last week, I began to feel an unusual pressure on the top of my head while meditating. I became frightened and stopped. What should I do?"

Sri Gurudev answered, "If you want the Guru to sit on your head, you must be prepared to hold his weight. Gurus are heavy, you know. All these days you have been imagining him sitting on the top of your head. Now that you feel his presence, why do you stop?"

Understanding what had happened, the young man asked, "When I feel the presence, should I continue to repeat my mantra?"

Gurudev said, "When someone is standing in your doorway waiting to come in, you say, "Come in, please come in."

Once that person has entered the room, will you continue to say, "Come in, come in?" No. You will offer the guest a seat and listen to what he or she has to say.

The mantra is like that–a calling or invocation. Once the presence is felt, there is no need to repeat the mantra. Just sit and listen to what it has to say to you."

Sri Gurudev Answers Questions about the Practice of Meditation

Q: While sitting, I experience tension in my back and neck, which hinders meditation. What can I do about it?

A: Well, the tension and the pain are mainly due to the stiffness of the body. The body is not fully relaxed. Either the body is too weak, or the body is still filled with toxins. So, you have to work on the body.

Make the body more relaxed. Purge out all the toxins that are already inside the body. Make it healthier. Then you won't feel the tension. Even after doing this, if you still feel a little tension, know that it is just common at the beginning.

Because in meditation there is a dynamic force developed in your own body, a static energy. It begins to rise up. Very often, you will feel the tension at the back of the neck or the back of the head. It is just natural. You should get used to that, because the power rises up. It goes to the brain.

After some practice, you will slowly get used to that force, and there won't be any pain. In fact, you will have a pleasant feeling about it. Just know that these sensations of tension and pain are common with everybody.

Everybody has to go through this. That shouldn't discourage you. It is the same with any new practice. Suppose you try bicycling for the first time. The following morning, you can't even get out of your bed. You have all kinds of pain everywhere. Or maybe you learned horseback riding. The first day you did it. The next day, you couldn't even walk straight. So these experiences, which we all have in common, can be gotten over easily.

Q: At a particular point when I am deep in meditation, I seem to be almost slipping off. I feel as though I'm dying, and I become frightened.

A: Yes, this does happen, but when I hear this it makes me very happy. Don't become frightened. This feeling occurs as a result of an automatic stoppage of breath. When the mind becomes still, the breathing will do the same.

If you experience retention of breath, no harm will come of it. This retention will not happen until your system is ready. It may even stop for a few minutes. And if you are deep enough in meditation, for hours. That is what you call *samadhi*, or super-consciousness.

Q: What should we do about intruding thoughts and desires during meditation?

A: One way is to treat the thoughts as an unwanted visitor. To give you an example, you are in your room and you are doing something intensely. All of a sudden, somebody walks in without any appointment. You just look at him through the corner of your eye and realize that this is not the time to see him.

How will you deal with him? There are three ways to deal with this intruder. One way is to respond immediately: "Why do you come without an appointment? Get out!" If you do this, he won't be going out happily. Instead, you will be making an enemy. He might bang the door behind him and even stand outside and shout.

You can't force him out. That would be a terrible thing to do. Likewise, don't try to force intruding thoughts out of your meditation. You will only create tension.

The second way is: You know he is there and you don't even look at him. You seem to be very busy, deeply involved in something. Even if he calls to you, your ears do not hear him. He will wait and wait, eventually coming to this realization: "I see that he is very busy; I will come again." Then, he will walk out.

On the other hand, if he is going to be adamant and tax your patience, then you say, "All right. Yes, sir? What can I do for you?" Here, you use the third method: analysis.

Let us examine the third method within the meditative situation. You are sitting and meditating and a desire to eat or go to the cinema comes in.

If you can't ignore or avoid it, take that and analyze it. "All right, you want to take me to the cinema? Fine; how many films have you seen all these days? With what benefit?

What is going to be different about this one over the others? What will benefit me more, the cinema or this meditation?" Analyze, question that and educate the desire itself.

"Well, I doubt that I'll get much benefit from the cinema."

"Okay. Then why can't you wait? I will certainly oblige you later. Let me finish meditating. Tomorrow we will go to the cinema."

Give in a little. Don't be adamant. It is necessary to give in a little, but not always. Treat your mind like a child who is naughty and wants this and that. Use your intelligence. Don't just give in to everything.

Pranayama:
Yogic Breathing Practices

This section is included because *pranayama* is an important aid to meditation. Patanjali, the father of Yoga philosophy, says that by *pranayama* the mind becomes clear and fit for concentration.

Prana is the vital or cosmic energy that causes any kind of motion—even the movement within an atom. Wherever you see movement, even a thought movement, it is caused by the *prana*, the energy or the force.

Electricity is *prana*. Your breathing is *prana*. Your digestion is *prana*. The different functions have different names, but they are all the same current or force, which is called *prana*. *Ayama* is control or regulation or mastery. *Pranayama* doesn't mean retention of *prana*; it is the control or regulation of *prana*. It is channeling the *prana* properly, directing it as you want.

Pranayama has three major sections: inhalation (*puraka*); exhalation (*rechaka*); and retention (*kumbhaka*). And there is another aspect where you do nothing; the breathing just stops.

When retention happens automatically without any effort, it is called *kevala kumbhaka*. This is our main aim: the breath should stop without any effort.

The main purpose of *pranayama* is to purify the system. *Pranayama* purifies the physical and vital body. Another important benefit is the calming and regulating of the mind.

Whenever you are upset, tense or worried, just do some slow, deep breathing with full attention on the breath, and you can easily bring the mind to a calm state.

The *prana*, or here the movement of the breath, and the movement of the mind go together. They are interdependent. If you regulate the *prana*, you have regulated the mind.

To give an example, suppose you are thinking seriously of a problem or trying to understand a passage that you are reading. Your mind is deeply concentrated on that.

All of a sudden, just stop that concentration and watch your breath. You will be surprised to see that you are not breathing, that your breathing has almost stopped. That is why you take a deep breath after such intense concentration; you want to make up for that temporary cessation of breath.

Actually, that is the reason why we meditate, to achieve the stillness of the *prana*. Even the movements of the mind are stopped, so, naturally, the breath is also stopped. There is complete stillness— mental, vital and physical.

That is why you are asked to sit quietly and steadily, without any movement of the body, not even the blinking of the eyelids.

So, there is no movement of the body, the breath or the thoughts. What is the achievement then? The achievement is no wastage or utilization of the electricity, or *prana* in your body.

The *prana* in your body comes to a standstill. In that stillness, as any technician knows, a kind of static energy is built up. In that static state, heat is produced. That is why if you sit quietly for some time and meditate deeply, you perspire profusely; this is because of the heat built up. And it is that heat that goes and works on the entire system. It is that heat that kindles certain dormant faculties, the psychic forces.

The major part of the force is called *kundalini*. It is not by violent movement that you rouse it, but by stopping all movements and building up that static heat within.

Unfortunately, many people think that *pranayama* means to breathe vehemently or to hold your breath as long as you can until your blood vessels burst. That is very dangerous.

Even though retention is given in the books, we should not aim for that in the beginning. It should come gradually. Most Yoga books give a 1:4:2 proportion. So, right away, a beginner starts: inhale ten, stop forty, exhale twenty. You may be able to do it a few times, but then you will get exhausted. One should never do that.

Practice a few rounds of *nadi suddhi* (alternate nostril breathing) before beginning meditation and you will soon experience its benefits. Breathe out slowly from the left nostril and then in through the some nostril; then switch, breathing out through the right nostril and then in through the same.

Switch again and continue in this manner. This is called *nadi suddhi,* or alternate nostril breathing. At a more advanced level, the breath is retained within the lungs after inhalation. This is called, *suka purvaka pranayama,* or the easy, comfortable breathing.

The scriptures say to practice *nadi suddhi* alone for several months and that, too, with proper habits in your life. Without following the yogic guidelines given for eating, drinking, sleeping, etc., your practice of *nadi suddhi* may even take six years.

You have to see and experience the benefits before you go on to retain the breath. Just by doing *nadi suddhi* alone the entire body will become light, and all the senses will be alert.

It is really detrimental to begin the 1:4:2 proportion without any discipline whatsoever. You may get a feeling of ecstasy, but it is not safe. People say they feel like they are fainting, but they get nice experiences.

Don't think that those experiences are going to help you. You may ultimately experience something that might put an end to all experiences.

So let us go slowly and gradually build up our capacity. Build your nerves first. *Nadi suddhi* means nerve purification. Before you hold your breath, your body must be strong enough. You should know your system.

It is something like pumping air into a weak tube–it might burst. So, when you go into *pranayama*, you must be very careful. If you really want the benefit, go slow and steady. Build up little by little.

Do *nadi suddhi* alone for some time– the time limit depends on the other disciplines you follow. If you follow all the other disciplines, like vegetarian diet, refraining from drinking or taking drugs, oversleeping, etc., then you will probably get the benefit within two or three months and can easily switch over to regular *pranayama*, the easy, comfortable breathing. If not, three months may extend to six months or a year.

Every time you breathe in, hold for a little while. Suppose you breathe in for ten counts, hold five counts, and exhale twenty counts. (The in-out proportion is 1:2. Retain little by little.) Then, try just a little bit of retention. But every time you go on to another step, see that you are able to perform at least forty or fifty breathings in a sitting. Even the fiftieth time, you should feel no strain.

When you can do *nadi suddhi* comfortably fifty times, then you are ready for a little retention. If you get tired after five or ten times, then you are not ready. Reduce the retention. Your exhalation must always be easy. If you find it difficult, you have retained longer than your capacity. Add little by little until you reach the 1:4:2 proportion. You need not increase beyond that but increase the number of *pranayamas*.

Pranayama alone is not the goal of our practice. Our main purpose is to calm and control the mind. Once you achieve the 1:4:2 ratio, you will be able to control the mind quickly. Then, occupy your mind in your *japa* (repetition of a mantra) or your meditation. There is no hurry with these things; do them gradually, with all perfection, following the discipline. Everything needs a little time and a particular method.

Eventually, once the mind is totally at rest and identification with the body and mind ceases, then you have become the witness, or what we call the pure Self. Ultimately, when you are able to keep up this awareness even in your day-to-day activities, you will have reached Self-realization. Then, as the master of your body and mind, you will walk the earth as an undisturbed sage.

For more in-depth instruction in pranayama, *please consult an Integral Yoga teacher or Swami Satchidananda's instructional CD, "The Breath of Life: Integral Yoga® Pranayama, Level I and Level II." For further instruction in meditation try the CD, "Guided Meditation" with Swami Satchidananda.*

Sri Swami Satchidananda

Sri Swami Satchidananda was one of the first Yoga masters to bring the classical Yoga tradition to the West. He taught Yoga postures to Americans, introduced them to meditation, vegetarian diet and a more compassionate lifestyle.

During this period of cultural awakening, iconic pop artist Peter Max and a small circle of his artist friends beseeched the Swami to extend his brief stop in New York City so they could learn from him the secret of finding physical, mental and spiritual health, peace and enlightenment.

Three years later, he led some half a million American youth in chanting *OM*, when he delivered the official opening remarks at the 1969 Woodstock Music and Art Festival and he became known as "the Woodstock Guru."

The distinctive teachings he brought with him blend the physical discipline of Yoga, the spiritual philosophy of Vedantic literature and the interfaith ideals he pioneered.

These techniques and concepts influenced a generation and spawned a Yoga culture that is flourishing today. Today, over twenty million Americans practice Yoga as a means for managing stress, promoting health, slowing down the aging process and creating a more meaningful life.

The teachings of Swami Satchidananda have spread into the mainstream and thousands of people now teach Yoga. Integral Yoga is the foundation for Dr. Dean Ornish's landmark work in reversing heart disease and Dr. Michael Lerner's noted Commonweal Cancer Help program.

Today, Integral Yoga Institutes, teaching centers and certified teachers throughout the United States and abroad offer classes and training programs in all aspects of Integral Yoga.

In 1979, Sri Swamiji was inspired to establish Satchidananda Ashram–Yogaville. Based on his teachings, it is a place where people of different faiths and backgrounds can come to realize their essential oneness.

One of the focal points of Yogaville is the Light Of Truth Universal Shrine (LOTUS). This unique interfaith shrine honors the Spirit that unites all the world religions, while celebrating their diversity. People from all over the world come there to meditate and pray.

Over the years, Sri Swamiji received many honors for his public service, including the Juliet Hollister Interfaith Award presented at the United Nations and in 2002 the U Thant Peace Award.

In addition, he served on the advisory boards of many Yoga, world peace and interfaith organizations. He is the author of many books on Yoga and is the subject of the documentary, *Living Yoga: The life and teachings of Swami Satchidananda.*

In 2002, he entered *Mahasamadhi* (a God-realized soul's conscious final exit from the body).

For more information, visit: www.IntegralYoga.org